HAL•LEONARD

EASY INSTRUMENTAL PLAY-ALONG

Audio Access Included

Visit www.halleonard.com/mylibrary

7979-0521-7678-2548

DISNEY FOR CELLO

CONTENTS

Audio Arrangements by Peter Deneff
Tracking, mixing, and mastering by BeatHouse Music

The following song is the property of:
Bourne Co.
Music Publishers
5 West 37th Street
New York, NY 10018

WHISTLE WHILE YOU WORK

ISBN 978-1-4803-5444-9

WALT DISNEY MUSIC COMPANY
WONDERLAND MUSIC COMPANY, INC.

DISTRIBUTED BY

HAL•LEONARD® CORPORATION

7777 W. BLUEMOUND RD. P.O. BOX 13819 MILWAUKEE, WI 53213

Visit Hal Leonard Online at
www.halleonard.com

THE BALLAD OF DAVY CROCKETT

from Walt Disney's DAVY CROCKETT

Words by TOM BLACKBURN
Music by GEORGE BRUNS

CAN YOU FEEL THE LOVE TONIGHT

from Walt Disney Pictures' THE LION KING

Music by ELTON JOHN
Lyrics by TIM RICE

CANDLE ON THE WATER
from Walt Disney's PETE'S DRAGON

Words and Music by AL KASHA
and JOEL HIRSCHHORN

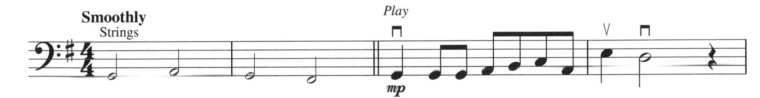

I JUST CAN'T WAIT TO BE KING

from Walt Disney Pictures' THE LION KING

Music by ELTON JOHN
Lyrics by TIM RICE

PART OF YOUR WORLD

from Walt Disney's THE LITTLE MERMAID

Music by ALAN MENKEN
Lyrics by HOWARD ASHMAN

Moderately fast

THE MEDALLION CALLS

from Walt Disney Pictures' PIRATES OF THE CARIBBEAN: THE CURSE OF THE BLACK PEARL

Music by KLAUS BADELT

WHISTLE WHILE YOU WORK

from Walt Disney's SNOW WHITE AND THE SEVEN DWARFS

Words by LARRY MOREY
Music by FRANK CHURCHILL

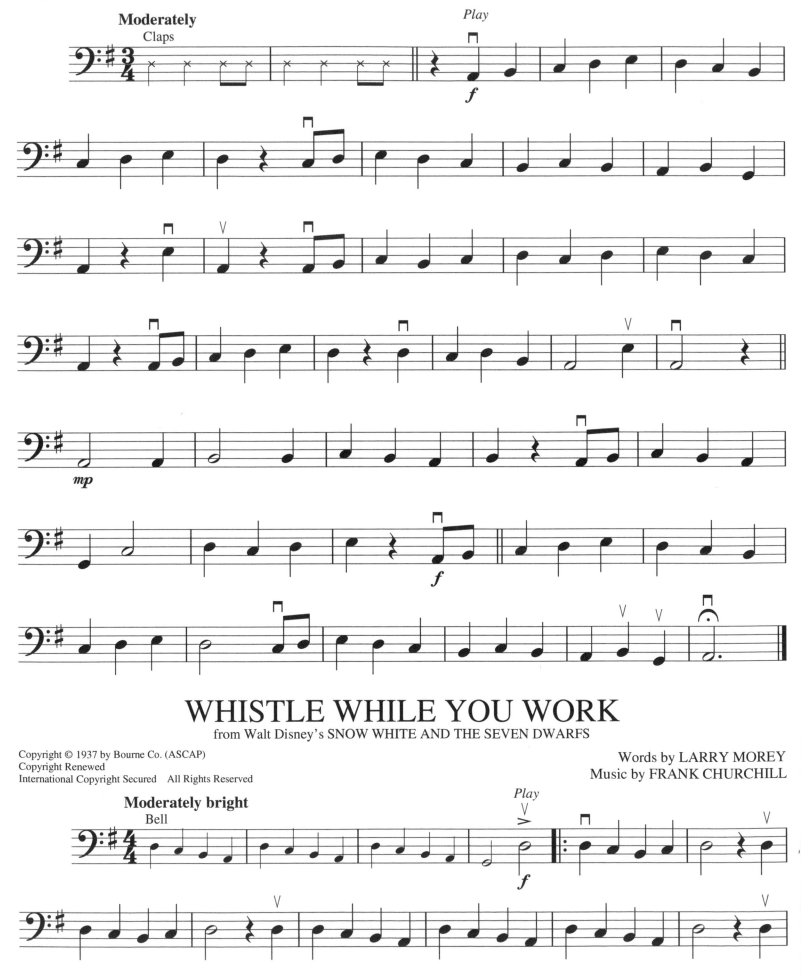

YOU'LL BE IN MY HEART
(Pop Version)

from Walt Disney Pictures' TARZAN™

Words and Music by
PHIL COLLINS

MICKEY MOUSE MARCH
from Walt Disney's THE MICKEY MOUSE CLUB

Words and Music by
JIMMIE DODD

YOU CAN FLY! YOU CAN FLY! YOU CAN FLY!
from Walt Disney's PETER PAN

Words by SAMMY CAHN
Music by SAMMY FAIN